FOUNDATION-PIECED
Double WEDDING RING QUILTS

SUMIKO MINEI

TRANSLATED BY
AYU OHTA

American Quilter's Society
P. O. Box 3290 • Paducah, KY 42002-3290
www.AmericanQuilter.com

Located in Paducah, Kentucky, the American Quilter's Society (AQS) is dedicated to promoting the accomplishments of today's quilters. Through its publications and events, AQS strives to honor today's quiltmakers and their work and to inspire future creativity and innovation in quiltmaking.

EXECUTIVE BOOK EDITOR: ANDI MILAM REYNOLDS
COPY EDITOR: LINDA BAXTER LASCO
TRANSLATION: AYU OHTA
ILLUSTRATIONS: MEGUMI MINEI
GRAPHIC DESIGN: ELAINE WILSON
COVER DESIGN: MICHAEL BUCKINGHAM
HOW-TO PHOTOGRAPHY: MEGUMI MINEI
QUILT PHOTOGRAPHY: CHARLES R. LYNCH

ATTENTION PHOTOCOPYING SERVICE: Please note the following—Publisher and author give permission to print pages 41–48, 50–57, and 59–61 for personal use only.

Additional copies of this book may be ordered from the American Quilter's Society, PO Box 3290, Paducah, KY 42002-3290, or online at www.AmericanQuilter.com.

Text © 2012, Author, Sumiko Minei
Artwork © 2012, American Quilter's Society

LIBRARY OF CONGRESS CATALOGING-IN-PUBLICATION DATA

Minei, Sumiko.
  Foundation-pieced double wedding ring quilts / by Sumiko Minei.
    64 pages cm
  Summary: "Sumiko Minei's 'Top Pressed Piecing' technique keeps the pattern on the right side of the fabric. Innovations to the traditional Double Wedding Ring pattern give this old stand-by design a fresh, modern look. The book includes full-size foundation patterns for 7 different projects and more than 100 step-by-step photos ensure sewing success"--Provided by publisher.
  ISBN 978-1-60460-030-8
  1. Patchwork--Patterns. 2. Double wedding ring quilts. I. Title.
  TT835.M56 2012
  746.46--dc23
                              2012025979

ON THE COVER: MEMORIES, detail. Full quilt on page 25.

Acknowledgments

I'd like to thank all the people who supported me to publish this book.

First, my sincere thanks to Jan Magee, editor-in-chief of *The Quilt Life* magazine, who was kind enough to introduce me to American Quilter's Society. Without her, I might still have no connection to AQS.

Thanks to Ayu Ohta, my longtime friend who has always supported me, I could concentrate on making quilts while she saw to all the communications between me and AQS, as well as translation. I wouldn't have thought about publishing my book with AQS if not for her.

Special thanks to these companies for providing products:

Brother Industries, Ltd., for their superb sewing machines;

Clover Mfg. Co., Ltd., for many useful tools from rotary cutters and mats to a special iron;

Fujix, Ltd., for their colorful fine threads; and

Moda Fabrics and Moda Japan for their wonderful fabrics.

Just as it was time to start making quilts for this book, the Great East Japan Earthquake occurred on March 11, 2011. I put my work aside and started the project "Quilt Aid" with Ayu Ohta and other friends to support the victims with quilts. We asked quilters around the world for quilts and received over 2,200 quilts; they encouraged the earthquake victims very much. We are very grateful for all the support shown Japan from many people in the world. Thanks to them, we are now working toward reconstruction in Tohoku.

This caused some delay in making quilts for this book, but the members in my quilting classes helped me a lot and made it possible to publish this book on time. My heartfelt thanks to Masako Kawasari, Junko Kawakami, Yoko Hitomi, Nobuko Hirata, Miki Ikutome, Ryoko Sakita, Kazumi Suetsugu, Rinko Tahara, Takako Nagasawa, Yuko Hashiguchi, Noriko Masuyama, Tokiko Mitsuyasu, Sueko Mitsuyasu, Kumiko Tsutsumi, Mitsuko Kamada, and Miho Yoshihara.

Special thanks to all the staff at American Quilter's Society who made this book so wonderful, and especially to Andi Reynolds, who was so helpful in every aspect.

My great thanks to my daughter, Megumi, who transformed my manuscript to data files to make my first self-published book. This current book wouldn't have been possible without her and my first book. After the Great East Japan Earthquake, my son had a baby boy, Yuki, who gave me new energy to keep making quilts until he's grown up.

Finally, my heartfelt thanks to my late husband. He allowed me to make quilts freely and admired my works. It was he who helped me get to where I am now.

Contents

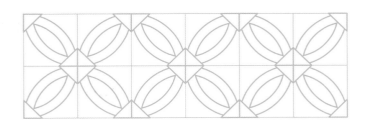

OPPOSITE PAGE: THANKS TO OUR ANCESTORS, detail.
Full quilt on page 27.

Author Permissions

Patterns in this book are traditional, but many of the methods of making them are my originals, therefore:

Using this book as a text book in quilting classes is welcome, but do not make photocopies of the patterns; each student should purchase the book to use the patterns.

Making photocopies from this book is allowed for personal use only for the person who purchased this book.

Sumiko Minei

Foreword

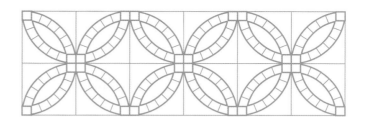

I wrote *Paper Foundation Piecing* (Patchwork Tsushin Co., Ltd., 1999), the first book on paper foundation piecing in Japan. In this technique you sew pieces of fabric onto a pattern-printed paper foundation and remove the paper after sewing.

Using paper foundations is a very convenient way of piecing because you don't have to bother about fabric grain, can use any material, and can easily sew fine points. But some people think it's confusing to sew from the wrong side of the pattern with the fabric facing away from you. Thinking about it, I developed a new method, Top Pressed Piecing, in which you sew on foundations but facing the fabric. I published a book about it in 2009. Even children can sew by this method and it has been well received.

At the same time I developed a method of piecing on paper foundations using embroidery software and an embroidery machine, both by Brother (see Resources). As I made Double Wedding Ring quilts this way and did demonstrations, people were admiring but wanted a way to use their regular sewing machines and asked for a book about my method.

In 2009, Brother began selling a circular attachment that made sewing Double Wedding Ring curves very easy. Of course, it is also easy to sew these patterns without this tool.

Double Wedding Ring is a popular pattern but challenging to draw. With this new book, you don't have to draw patterns and you can use my easy sewing technique.

This pattern was popular in the 1920s and 1930s during the Great Depression in the United States. Usually scraps were used in the rings with white fabric for the background. In the sample quilts, you will see how this color scheme has been updated and made modern.

I hope you'll use your favorite colors and make wonderful rings by this method.

Sumiko Minei
May 2012
Tokyo

OPPOSITE PAGE: MEMORIES, detail. Full quilt on page 25.

Technique

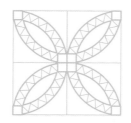

TOOLS

Chalk liner and/or pencil
Circular attachment (optional—see page 23)
Fabric glue stick or removable glue stick
Fusible tape (5mm or ³⁄₁₆" or ¼")
Iron
Pins
Rotary mat, ruler, and cutter
Red pencil
Small scissors for close trimming
Thread
    Sewing to match background fabric
    Contrasting or decorative thread to satin stitch
Tweezers

BASIC METHOD

I use the Grape Peel pattern with traditional curved corners to demonstrate the basic foundation piecing method. Specific technique changes for Double Wedding Ring and Indian Wedding Ring follow later in the chapter. I also include two corner variations—square and triangle—that may be used with any pattern except the Connecting Squares pattern, which does not call for corners. It is best to read all the way through the directions, gallery, and patterns to avoid confusion.

See pages 38–39 for fabric requirements. See pages 50–57 for foundation piecing patterns.

Use thread that matches the background fabric to sew the curved lines. I used satin stitch for the decorative stitching, but you can use other stitches such as a blanket stitch or appliqué stitch. Use any color you like for the decorative stitching. For satin stitching, I set my machine at stitch width 3, length 0.3 but if this doesn't fit you, please find the best setting for your machine.

OPPOSITE PAGE: THANKS TO THE QUILTERS, detail. Full quilt on page 35.

Using One Background Fabric – Grape Peel Pattern

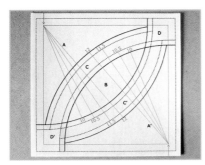

1. Prepare a paper foundation that is 5mm (¼") larger than the blue dotted line around the pattern.

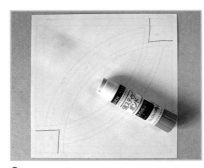

2. Draw the red line on the back of the paper foundation. Dab fabric glue on some points on the back side of the paper. *

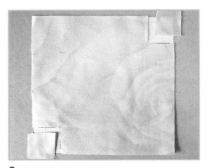

3. Hold the background fabric in place by pressing it, right side up, against the glue side of the foundation. Cut away the fabric from the two red line-marked corners.

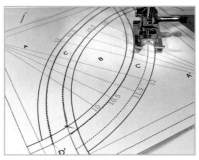

4. Sew on the 10.5cm (4⅛") and 11.5cm (4½") lines. Start sewing in the seam allowance to secure stitches when removing the foundation.

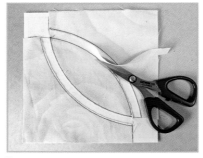

5. Trim away the fabric between the sewn lines.

6. Cut and fuse 5mm (¼") tape to the trimmed area.

7. Fold the ring fabric C and C' in half and snip 1cm (⅜") in the center.

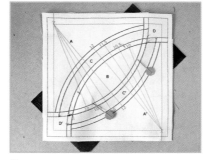

8. Pin the ring fabric C and C' on the wrong side of the paper foundation.

9. Cut away the C and C' from the marked corners (do not cut away the foundation paper).

If you put too much glue, some paper may remain on fabric when you remove paper.

Using One Background Fabric – Grape Peel Pattern (continued)

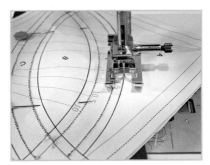

10. Sew the 12cm (4¾") lines.

11. After sewing the lines in step 10.

12. Cut away the extra fabric around the sewing lines. Trim very close to the stitching. Do not cut the foundation fabric.

13. Iron fusible web tape on the seam allowances. Place corner fabrics D and D' and pin.

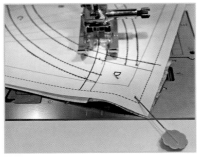

14. Sew on the two inside black lines.

15. After sewing the lines in step 14.

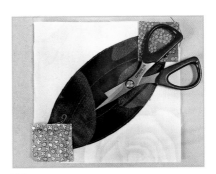

16. Trim away the extra fabric inside the ring and from the seam allowances of the corner fabric.

17. After trimming in step 16.

18. Satin stitch the outside ring lines.

Using One Background Fabric – Grape Peel Pattern (continued)

19. Satin stitch the inside ring lines.

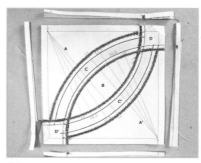

20. Trim the block along the dotted blue lines.

21. Tear the paper foundation away from the finished block.

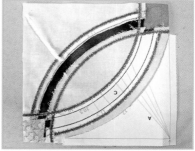

22. When tearing the paper, place your fingernail on the seam and gently pull off the paper. ◆

Using Two Background Fabrics – Grape Peel Pattern

1. Glue fabrics A and A' on the back of the paper pattern.

2. Sew on the 11.5cm (4½") lines.

3. Cut off the extra fabric.

4. Position fabric B; be sure it covers all curved lines. Glue in place.

5. Sew on the 10.5cm (4⅛") lines.

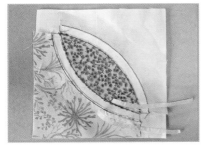

6. Cut off the extra fabric.

7. Glue fabric C.

8. Sew on the 10cm (3⅞") and 12cm (scant 4¾") lines and cut off the extra fabric.

9. Glue fabric C'.

10. Sew on the 10cm (3⅞") and 12cm (scant 4¾") lines and cut off the extra fabric.

11. Do not cut off the seam allowance shown inside the circle in the photo.

12. Position the corner fabric and finish the pattern. ◆

METHOD VARIATIONS

Sewing the Double Wedding Ring Pattern

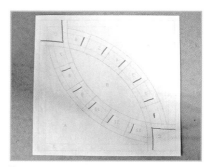

1. Draw the red lines and numbers on the back side of the paper pattern.

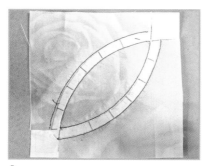

2. Follow steps 2–5 for Grape Peel on page 12.

3. Place fabrics 1 and 2 right-sides together. Place them on the red line between numbers 1 and 2.

4. Pin.

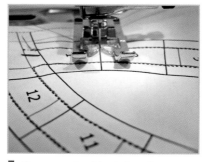

5. Sew on the black line between numbers 1 and 2.

6. Iron fabrics 1 and 2 open. This makes the block neat.

7. Cut off the extra fabric.

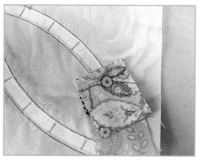

8. Position fabric 3 on fabric 2 right-sides together. Pin. Sew on the black line between numbers 2 and 3. Press.

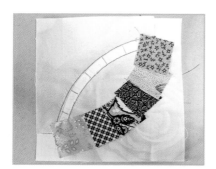

9. Continue placing and sewing through fabric 6.

Sewing the Double Wedding Ring Pattern (continued)

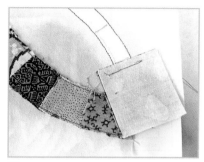

10. Sew on the 10cm (3⅞") and 12cm (scant 4¾") lines as in the Grape Peel pattern (page 13).

11. Cut off the extra fabric.

12. Repeat steps 3–7 for fabrics 7–12.

13. Cut off the extra fabric.

14. Sew the corner fabric(s) as in steps 13–15 of the Grape Peel pattern (page 13).

15. Finished block. ◆

Sewing the Indian Wedding Ring Pattern

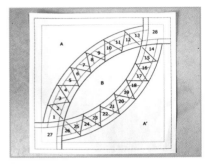

1. Prepare a paper foundation that is 5mm (¼") larger than the blue dotted line around the pattern.

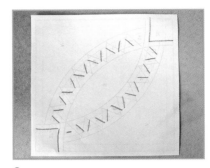

2. Draw the red lines and numbers on the back side of the paper pattern.

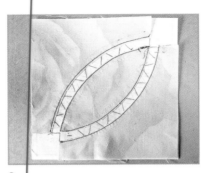

3. Follow steps 2–5 for the Grape Peel pattern (page 12).

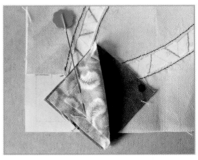

4. Place fabrics 1 and 2 right-sides together. Place them on the red line between numbers 1 and 2.

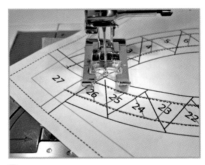

5. Pin. Sew on the black line between numbers 1 and 2.

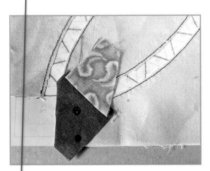

6. Iron fabrics 1 and 2 open. Cut off the extra fabric outside the red lines.

7. Position fabric 3 on fabric 2, right-sides together. Pin. Sew from the right side on the black line between numbers 2 and 3.

8. Take care in placing the fabrics.

9. Sew fabrics 4 – 13 in the same way.

Sewing the Indian Wedding Ring Pattern (continued)

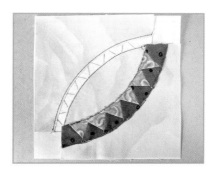

10. Sew on the 10cm (3⅞") and 12cm (scant 4¾") lines and cut off the extra fabric.

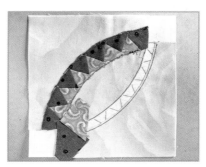

11. Place fabrics 14 and 15 right-sides together, position on the red line between numbers 14 and 15, pin, and sew on the black line between numbers 14 and 15.

12. Sew fabrics 16–26 the same way and sew on the 10cm (3⅞") and 12cm (scant 4¾") lines.

13. Cut off the extra fabric and sew the corner fabric.

14. Satin stitch the outside ring lines. ◆

Sewing the Connecting Corners Pattern

1. Snip the background fabric A as shown in the photo.

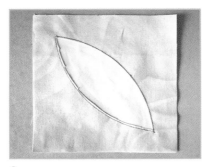

2. Sew the 11cm (4⁵⁄₁₆") lines. Insert the scissors through the snip and cut out the center.

3. Position fabric B and sew on the 11.5cm (4½") lines. Cut off the extra fabric.

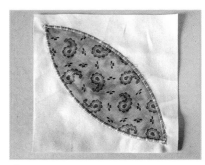

4. Sew the curved lines with your favorite stitch. ◆

Sewing Any Pattern with Square Corners

1. Follow steps 1–12 for One Background Fabric – Grape Peel Pattern (pages 12–13).

2. Satin stitch the outside ring lines.

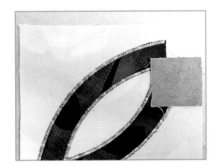

3. Iron fusible tape on the back of the corner squares. Position them.

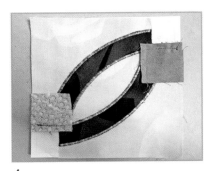

4. Flip and sew from the pattern printed side.

5. Draw the appliqué lines and fold the fabric along those lines.

6. Appliqué the squares on the folded line. ◆

Sewing Any Pattern with Triangle Corners

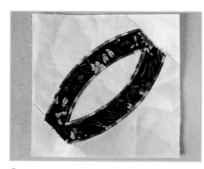

1. Follow steps 1–12 for the One Background Fabric – Grape Peel Pattern (pages 12–13).

2. Stitch on the curved lines with your favorite stitch.

3. Position triangle fabrics on the red line. Flip and sew them from the pattern printed side. ◆

Using a Circular Attachment

It is quite possible to make beautiful Double Wedding Ring quilts without a special tool, but I use the circular attachment for my machine (Brother). It is easy to use, makes it convenient to sew curved lines, and makes a neat satin stitch.

Ask your sewing machine dealer about a similar tool.

Instead of sewing a satin stitch, consider using a blading foot or cording foot to sew a fancy stitch.

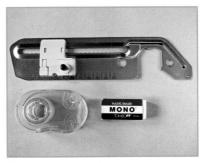

1. Circular attachment, tape, and eraser. To avoid making the hole larger, put a piece of tape on the hole.

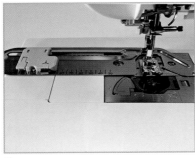

2. Attach the tool according to the manual.

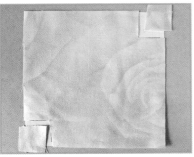

3. Glue the background fabric on the paper foundation like the Grape Peel pattern (pages 12–14).

4. Pin the corner of the foundation as shown in the photo. It would be easy to do so on an eraser.

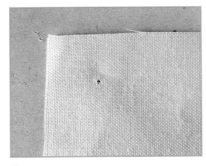

5. The pin makes a hole on the fabric, too.

6. Stretch the fabric by hand because if the fabric sags, you can't sew accurately.

7. Adjust the gauge of the circular attachment and sew it facing the fabric.

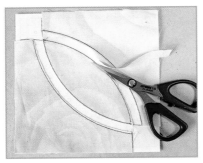

8. Cut off the extra fabric. ◆

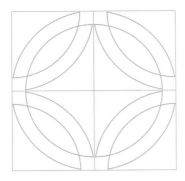

Gallery

Editor's note: *Individual sewing styles, the shrinkage from satin stitching, and the amount of quilting will affect the size of your quilt, even though you start out with these very accurate foundation piecing patterns. Even so, these dimensions from the actual quilts will give you a good idea of what you should expect from your project.*

Remember that including borders is a matter of individual taste, and these can be adjusted in number, style, and width to meet your needs. Numbers here indicate finished widths. Note that the binding was included in "actual quilt size" measurements, and for every quilt, the binding measured a generous ⅜" but never quite ½". Please adjust your quilt planning accordingly.

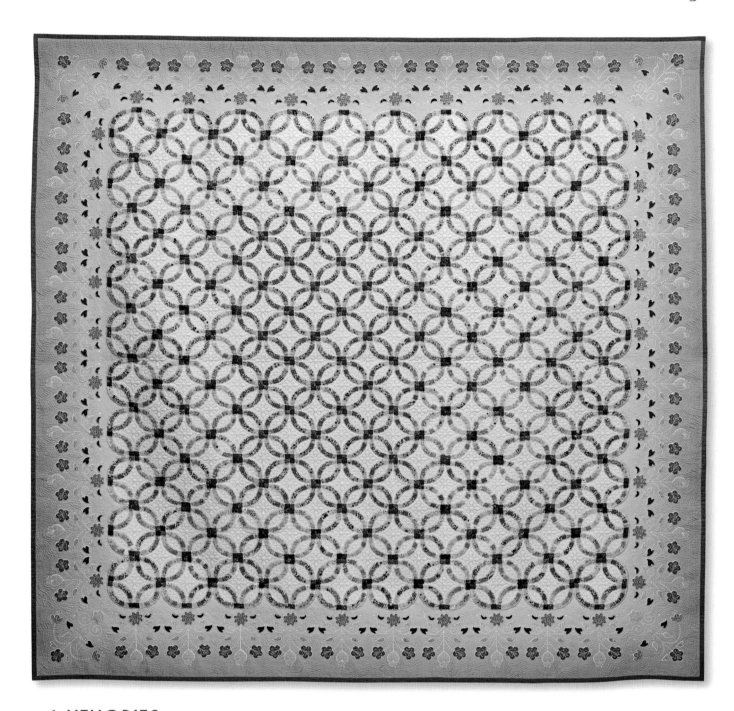

1 MEMORIES
Sumiko Minei, 2007

Double Wedding Ring with Square Corners
77½" x 77½"
- ◆ 3" finished blocks (Reduce the pattern on page 55 by 64% to make a 3½" unfinished block.)
- ◆ 20 blocks by 20 blocks
- ◆ 60⅝" x 60⅝" center
- ◆ 8½" wide border with appliqués

I was too busy working to make my double wedding ring quilt for years after I married. After my husband passed away, I made this quilt, remembering when I met him and our newlywed years. I wish I could show this to him. He would admire it.

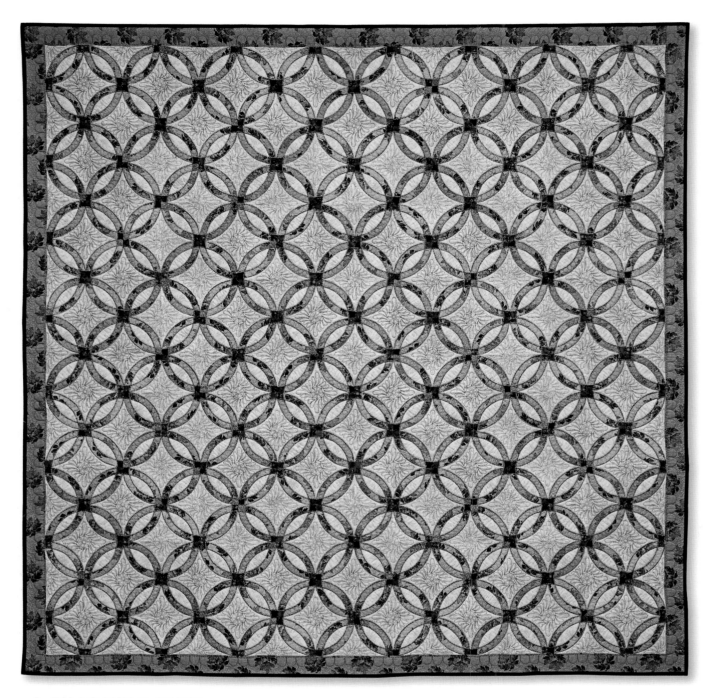

2 ENJOYING WINE

Sumiko Minei, 2009

Grape Peel with Traditional Corners
74" x 75½"
- ◆ 4¾" finished blocks (pattern on page 50 is 100%)
- ◆ 16 blocks by 16 blocks
- ◆ 70" x 71½" center
- ◆ 2" border

In Japan we enjoy sake in each season—winter for snow, spring for cherry blossoms, summer for fresh greens, and fall for colored leaves. I'm really happy enjoying wine and talking with my friends during long fall nights.

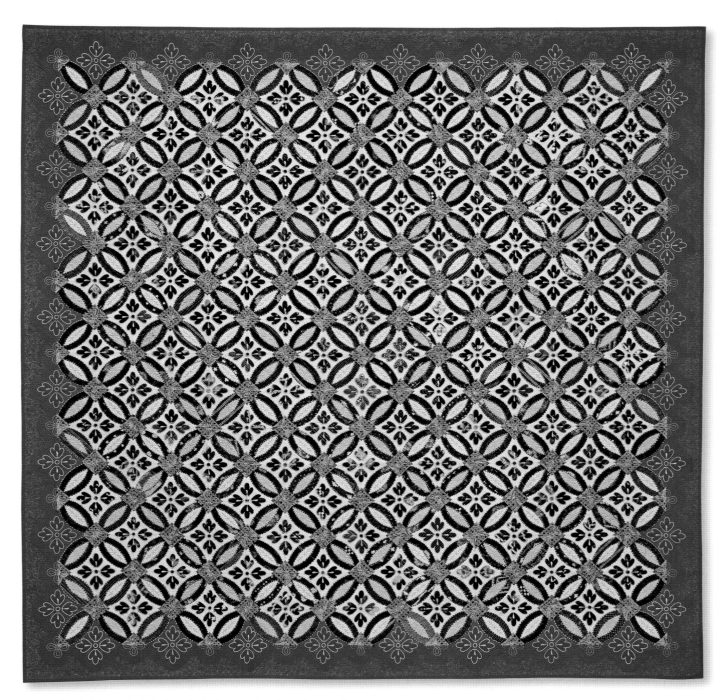

3 THANKS TO OUR ANCESTORS
Sumiko Minei, 2010

Grape Peel with Triangle Corners
80⅜" x 79¾"
- ◆ 4¾" finished blocks (pattern on page 52 is 100%)
- ◆ 16 blocks by 16 blocks
- ◆ 72" x 71" center
  border width varies but is 7" at the widest point

I created my original pattern from traditional ones. This is different from the Japanese shippo pattern (Seven Treasures) and the American Double Wedding Ring pattern. When I cut old fabrics, I feel myself straightening up by thinking of our ancestors and their lives. Thanks to them, we can live peacefully now. It is our responsibility to pass the treasures our ancestors left us to the next generation.

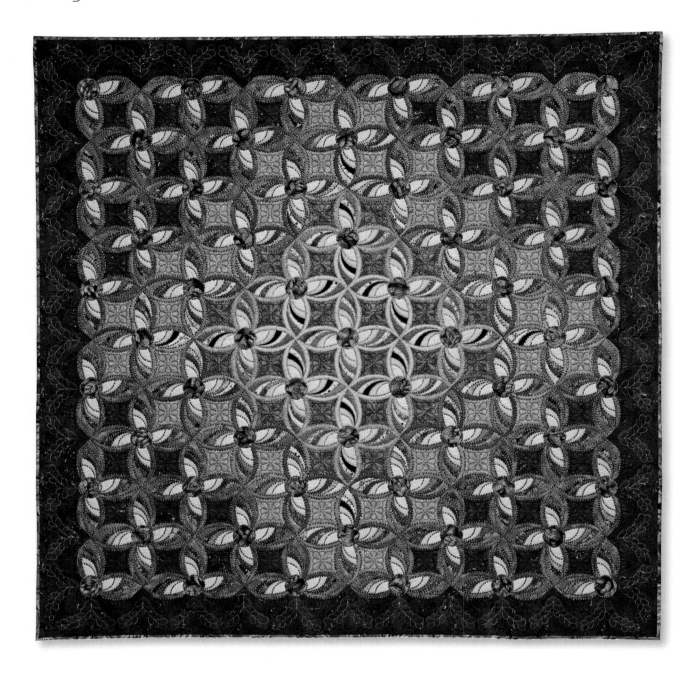

4 THE BLESSINGS OF THE EARTH

Tokiko Mitsuyasu, 2010

Connecting Corners

76" x 76"

- 4¾" finished blocks (pattern on page 53 is 100%)
- 10 blocks by 10 blocks
- 66¾" x 67¼" center
- circle raw-edge appliqués are 2¾"
- border width varies but is 6⅛" at the widest point

This is a variation of the Connecting Corners pattern. I made this quilt while imagining flowers grown up by the blessings of the Sun and Mother Earth.

5 TO MY NEXT DREAM
Nobuko Hirata, 2010

Double Wedding Ring with Traditional Corners
51½" x 53"

◆ 4¾" finished blocks (pattern on page 54 is 100%)
◆ 8 blocks across by 9 blocks down
◆ 43½" x 44⅝" center
◆ border is 3½"

While I supported my sons who were trying hard to achieve their dreams, my childhood dream popped up in my mind. I thought, "Now my sons are grown up and if I can spare time for myself, it would be nice to follow my dream, which I've come close to giving up. If I can find a new me, I may go to the next stage." While making this quilt, expectations and anxieties intermingled in my heart. It was not easy for me to make this paper-foundation pieced pattern, which was my first attempt at the technique, but doing it gave me the confidence to go ahead with my dream.

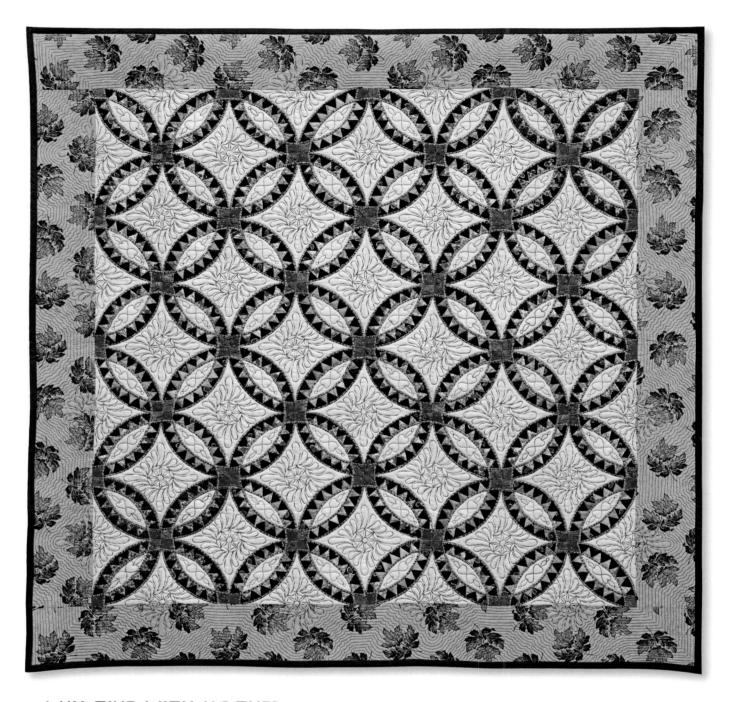

6 MY TIME WITH MOTHER

Yoko Hitomi, 2010

Indian Wedding Ring with Traditional Corners
44⅛" x 43⅜"

- ◆ 4¾" finished blocks (pattern on page 56 is 100%)
- ◆ 8 blocks by 8 blocks
- ◆ 35⅝" x 35⅛" center
- ◆ border is 3¾"

My late mother had beloved pets—"Chaco," a Siamese; and "Akubi," a Chihuahua. Thinking of the time I spent with my mother, I made her this quilt to tell her these pets are still well looked-after.

7 SPRING: APRIL

Sumiko Minei and Tong Tong Quilt members, 2011

Grape Peel with Square Corners

50¾" x 60⅛"

- ◆ 4¾" finished blocks (pattern on page 51 is 100%)
- ◆ 8 blocks across by 10 blocks down
- ◆ 36¾" x 46" center
- ◆ inner border is ¾"
- ◆ outer border is 5½"

In spring, flowers start blooming and warm sunshine makes us happy. It's also a season of new starts for students and workers. Even rains are appreciated, especially for farmers to sow seeds. Thinking of all of these, I expressed Japanese spring in this quilt.

8 2011.3.11: TSUNAMI

Sumiko Minei and Tong Tong Quilt members, 2011

Grape Peel with Triangle Corners

47⅛" x 56⅝"

◆ 4¾" finished blocks (pattern on page 52 is 100%)
◆ 8 blocks across by 10 blocks down
◆ 36⅜" x 45½"
◆ inner border is ⅝"
◆ outer border is 4⅜"

This design is called wa-chigai or shippo in Japan. Entwined circles symbolize trust, eternity, happiness, and link. They represent "many hands can do what cannot be done by one person." After experiencing the tragedies of tsunami and nuclear accidents on March 11, 2011, I made this quilt, hoping Japan will come alive again.

9 FIREPLACE
Sueko Mitsuyasu, 2011

Grape Peel with Triangle Corners
38⅜" x 46⅜"
- ◆ 4¾" finished blocks (pattern on page 52 is 100%)
- ◆ 8 blocks across by 10 blocks down

When I made the tsunami quilt with my friends, some of the sunflower prints were left. The fabric reminded me of a warm fire in the fireplace in the center of the family room.

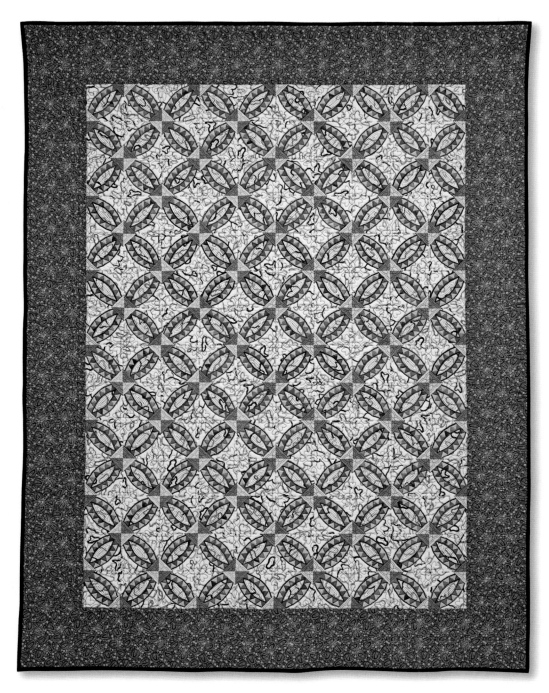

10 SALTATION
Sumiko Minei and Tong Tong Quilt members, 2011

Indian Wedding Ring with Square Corners
59 1/4" x 78¾"
- 4¾" finished blocks (pattern on page 57 is 100%)
- 10 blocks across by 14 blocks down
- 44⅝" x 63⅝" center
- border is 7"

Huge heaps of rubble still remain in the tsunami-hit regions. But even there flowers bloom and fresh leaves grow out of broken trees. 2011 was the year when I realized the life of the earth.

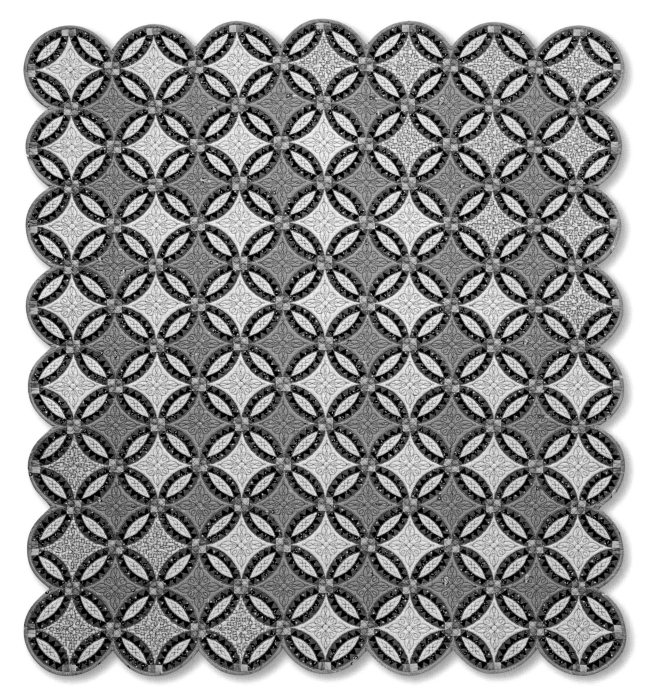

11 THANKS TO THE QUILTERS
Sumiko Minei and Tong Tong Quilt members, 2011

Indian Wedding Ring with Square Corners
63½" x 72"
- 4¾" finished blocks (pattern on page 57 is 100%)
- 14 blocks across by 16 blocks down

When I asked for baby quilts for the victims of the great earthquake, 2,200 quilts came from around the world. The quilts gave power to the children, parents, and people who lost houses with the message that they are not alone. This is our thanks to the quilters who supported Japan.

Yardage by Pattern

These fabric requirements are generous. They assume a quilt center of 4¾" x 4¾" (12cm x 12 cm) finished blocks set 8 by 12, or approximately 38" x 57" (96cm x 144cm), and fabric that has a useable width of 40" (100cm).

If you wish to replicate the Gallery quilts (pages 25–35), please see the pattern pages for additional information and adjust your yardage accordingly.

If you use pieced fabric for Piece B, such as Log Cabin or Crazy Patch, you create a different look. Adjust your yardage accordingly.

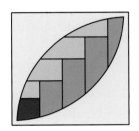

Piece B
Log Cabin

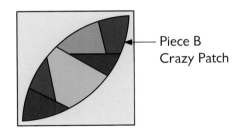

Piece B
Crazy Patch

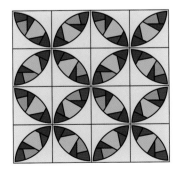

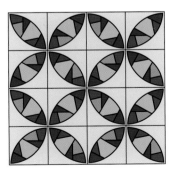

OPPOSITE PAGE: ENJOYING WINE, detail.
Full quilt on page 26.

PATTERN: GRAPE PEEL WITH TRADITIONAL CORNERS

Fabric	Yardage	Total
A and A'	2¾ yards or 1⅜ yards each	2¾ yards
B	1 yard	1 yard
C and C'	1½ yards or ¾ yard each	1½ yard
D	¾ yard	¾ yard
		6 yards

PATTERN: GRAPE PEEL WITH SQUARE CORNERS

Fabric	Yardage	Total
A and A'	2¾ yards or 1⅜ yards each	2¾ yards
B	1 yard	1 yard
C and C'	1½ yards or ¾ yard each	1½ yard
D	¾ yard	¾ yard
		6 yards

PATTERN: GRAPE PEEL WITH TRIANGLE CORNERS

Fabric	Yardage	Total
A and A'	2¾ yards or 1⅜ yards each	2¾ yards
B	1 yard	1 yard
C and C'	1½ yards or ¾ yard each	1½ yard
D	1½ yards	1½ yards
		6¾ yards

PATTERN: CONNECTING CORNERS

Fabric	Yardage	Total
A and A'	2¾ yards or 1⅜ yards each	2¾ yards
B	2¼ yards	2¼ yards
		5 yards
Appliqués at intersections (optional; 52 needed)	½ yard (52 circles 2¾" finished)	**5½ yards**

PATTERN: DOUBLE WEDDING RING WITH TRADITIONAL CORNERS

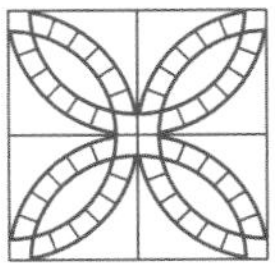

Fabric	Yardage	Total
A and A'	2¾ yards or 1⅜ yards each	2¾ yards
B	1 yard	1 yard
Pieces 1–12	¼ yard each	6½ yards
Pieces 13, 14	½ yard	½ yard
		10¾ yards

PATTERN: DOUBLE WEDDING RING WITH SQUARE CORNERS

Fabric	Yardage	Total
A and A'	2¾ yards or 1⅜ yards each	2¾ yards
B	1 yard	1 yard
Pieces 1–12	¼ yard each	6½ yards
Pieces 13, 14	½ yard	½ yard
		10¾ yards

PATTERN: INDIAN WEDDING RING WITH TRADITIONAL CORNERS

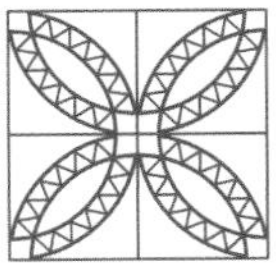

Fabric	Yardage	Total
A and A'	2¾ yards or 1⅜ yards each	2¾ yards
B	1 yard	1 yard
Fabrics 1–26	¼ yard of each fabric	6½ yards
Fabrics 27–28	½ yard of each fabric	1 yard
C (corners)		
		11¼ yards

PATTERN: INDIAN WEDDING RING WITH SQUARE CORNERS

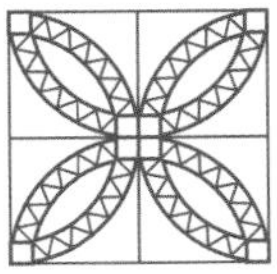

Fabric	Yardage	Total
A and A'	2¾ yards or 1⅜ yards each	2¾ yards
B	1 yard	1 yard
Fabrics 1–26	¼ yard of each fabric	6½ yards
Fabrics 27–28	½ yard of each fabric	1 yard
		11¼ yards

Worksheets for Coloring

GRAPE PEEL WITH TRADITIONAL CORNERS

GRAPE PEEL WITH SQUARE CORNERS

GRAPE PEEL WITH TRIANGLE CORNERS

CONNECTING CORNERS

DOUBLE WEDDING RING WITH TRADITIONAL CORNERS

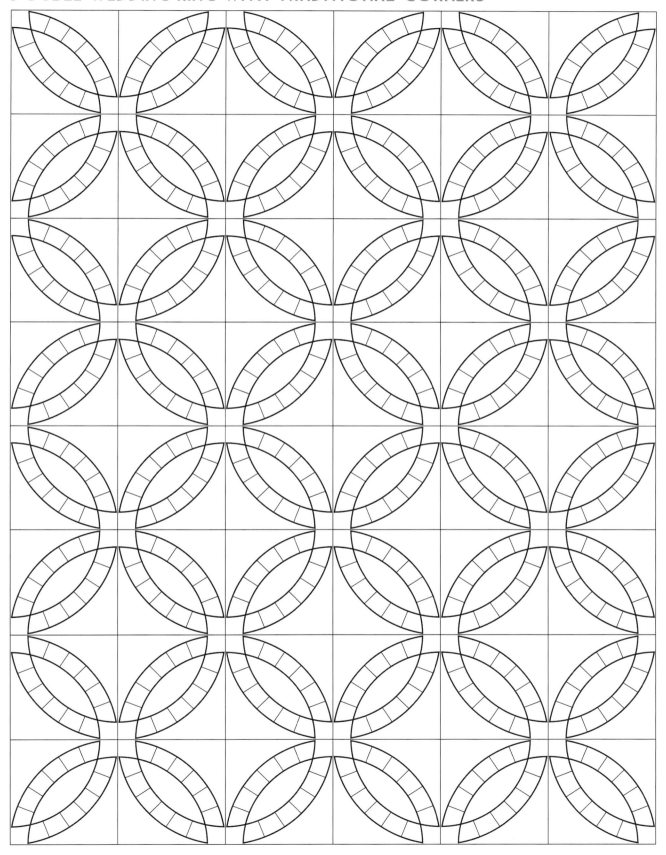

DOUBLE WEDDING RING WITH SQUARE CORNERS

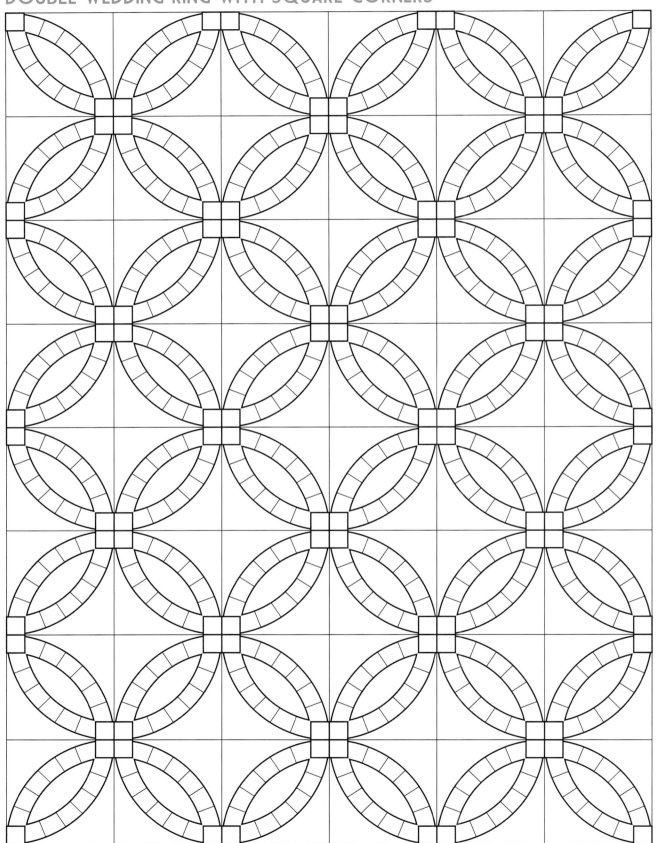

INDIAN WEDDING RING WITH TRADITIONAL CORNERS

INDIAN WEDDING RING WITH SQUARE CORNERS

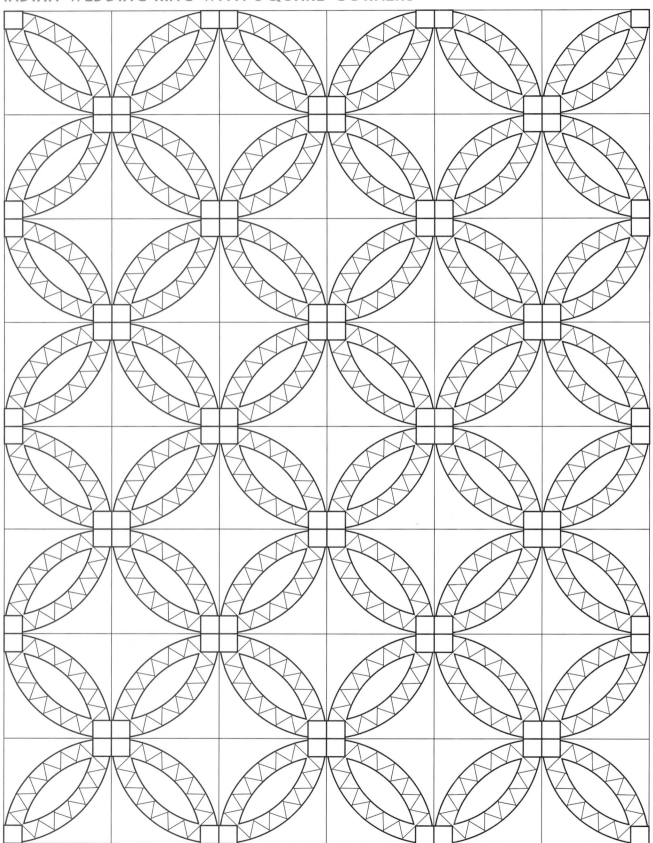

Foundation Piecing Patterns

FOUNDATION PIECING PATTERN KEY:

—————— Sewing line

———— Finish line

------------- Line including seam allowance

———— Fabric guideline

⊓⊓⊓⊓⊓⊓ Whip stitch

Note: The conversion from metric to imperial measurements is not exact. If you can use my original metric measurements rather than the converted inches, your work will probably be more accurate.

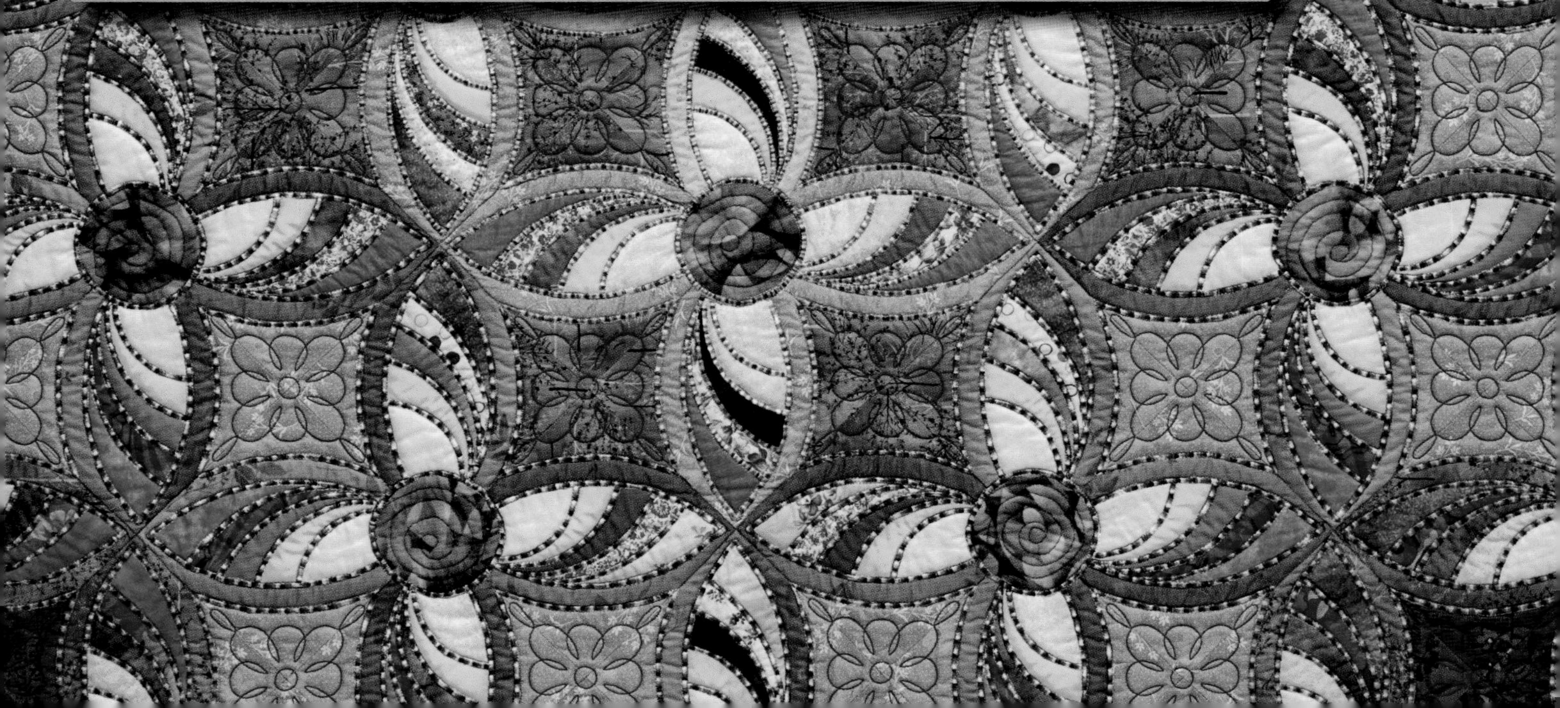

THIS PAGE: THE BLESSINGS OF THE EARTH, detail. Full quilt on page 28.

GRAPE PEEL WITH TRADITIONAL CORNERS

The place you put the circular attachment pin.

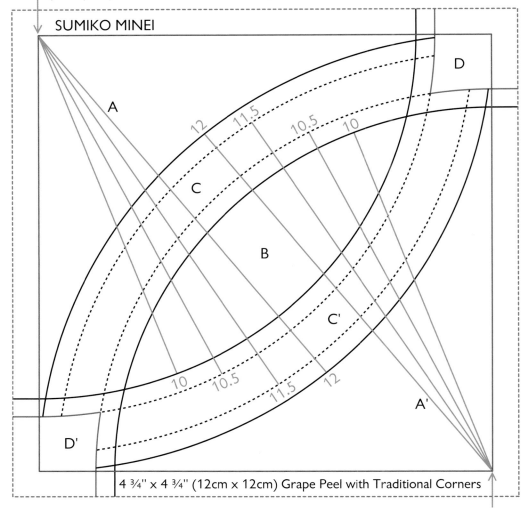

SUMIKO MINEI

A

12   11.5   10.5   10

D

C

B

C'

10   10.5   11.5   12

A'

D'

4 ¾" x 4 ¾" (12cm x 12cm) Grape Peel with Traditional Corners

The place you put the circular attachment pin.

◆ When you use different colors for each piece:

A ...... $\frac{5¾" \times 5¾"}{2}$ ($\frac{14.5cm \times 14.5cm}{2}$) 1 piece

A' ..... $\frac{5¾" \times 5¾"}{2}$ ($\frac{14.5cm \times 14.5cm}{2}$) 1 piece

B ...... 2" x 5⅛" (5cm x 13cm) 1 piece

C ...... 2" x 6¼" (5cm x 16cm) 1 piece

C' ..... 2" x 6¼" (5cm x 16cm) 1 piece

D ...... 1⅝" sq (4cm x 4cm) 1 piece

D' ..... 1⅝" sq (4cm x 4cm) 1 piece

◆ When you use the same colors for some parts:

When you use the same color for A, A' and B:

.................5¾" sq (14.5cm x 14.5cm) 1 piece

When you use the same color for C & C':

..........3⅜" x 6¼" (8.5cm x 16cm) 1 piece

When you use the same color for D & D':

....................1⅝" sq (4cm x 4cm) 2 pieces

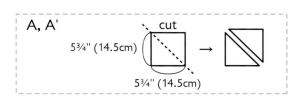

A, A'

cut

5¾" (14.5cm)

5¾" (14.5cm)

GRAPE PEEL WITH SQUARE CORNERS

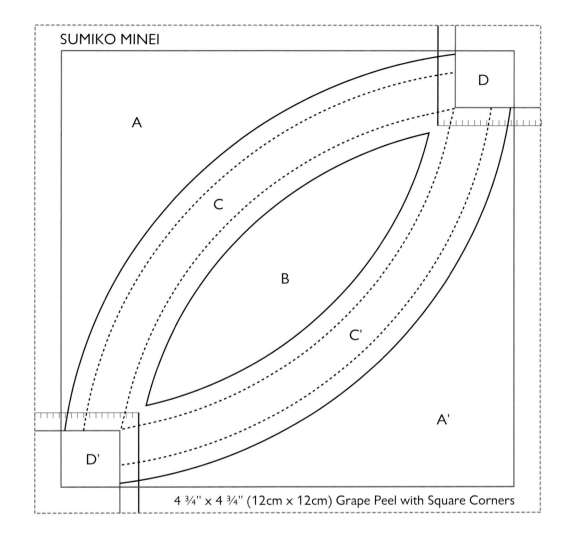

SUMIKO MINEI

4 ¾" x 4 ¾" (12cm x 12cm) Grape Peel with Square Corners

◆ When you use different colors for each piece:

A ...... $\dfrac{5\frac{3}{4}" \times 5\frac{3}{4}"}{2}$ ($\dfrac{14.5cm \times 14.5cm}{2}$) 1 piece

A' ..... $\dfrac{5\frac{3}{4}" \times 5\frac{3}{4}"}{2}$ ($\dfrac{14.5cm \times 14.5cm}{2}$) 1 piece

B ...... 2" x 5⅛" (5cm x 13cm) 1 piece

C ...... 2" x 6¼" (5cm x 16cm) 1 piece

C' ..... 2" x 6¼" (5cm x 16cm) 1 piece

D ...... 1⅝" sq (4cm x 4cm) 1 piece

D' ..... 1⅝" sq (4cm x 4cm) 1 piece

◆ When you use the same colors for some parts:

When you use the same color for A, A' and B:

.................5¾" sq (14.5cm x 14.5cm) 1 piece

When you use the same color for C & C':

...........3⅜" x 6¼" (8.5cm x 16cm) 1 piece

When you use the same color for D & D':

....................1⅝" sq (4cm x 4cm) 2 pieces

GRAPE PEEL WITH TRIANGLE CORNERS

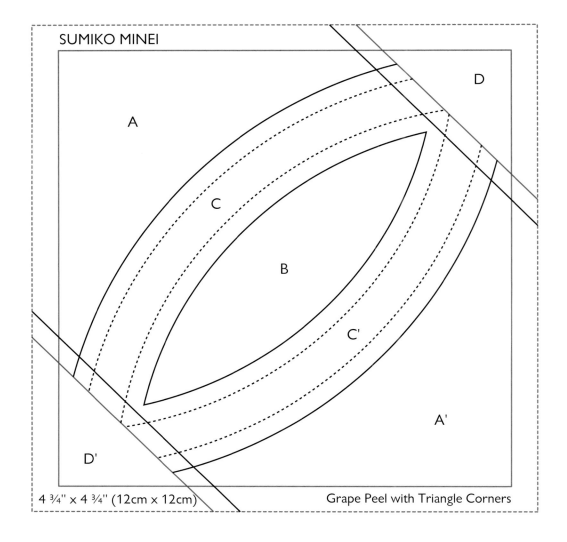

SUMIKO MINEI

A

D

C

B

C'

A'

D'

4 ¾" x 4 ¾" (12cm x 12cm)

Grape Peel with Triangle Corners

◆ When you use different colors for each piece:

A ...... $\frac{5¾" \times 5¾"}{2}$ ($\frac{14.5cm \times 14.5cm}{2}$) 1 piece

A' ..... $\frac{5¾" \times 5¾"}{2}$ ($\frac{14.5cm \times 14.5cm}{2}$) 1 piece

B ...... 2" x 5⅛" (5cm x 13cm) 1 piece

C ...... 2" x 5" (5cm x 12.5cm) 1 piece

C' ..... 2" x 5" (5cm x 12.5cm) 1 piece

D ...... $\frac{3⅛" \times 3⅛"}{2}$ ($\frac{8cm \times 8cm}{2}$) 1 piece

D' ..... $\frac{3⅛" \times 3⅛"}{2}$ ($\frac{8cm \times 8cm}{2}$) 1 piece

◆ When you use the same colors for some parts:

When you use the same color for A, A' and B:

.................5¾" sq (14.5cm x 14.5cm) 1 piece

When you use the same color for C & C':

.........3⅜" x 5" (8.5cm x 12.5cm) 1 piece

When you use the same color for D & D':

.....................$\frac{3⅛" \times 3⅛"}{2}$ ($\frac{8cm \times 8cm}{2}$) 1 piece

A, A'
D, D'

cut

5¾" (14.5cm)

5¾" (14.5cm)

CONNECTING CORNERS

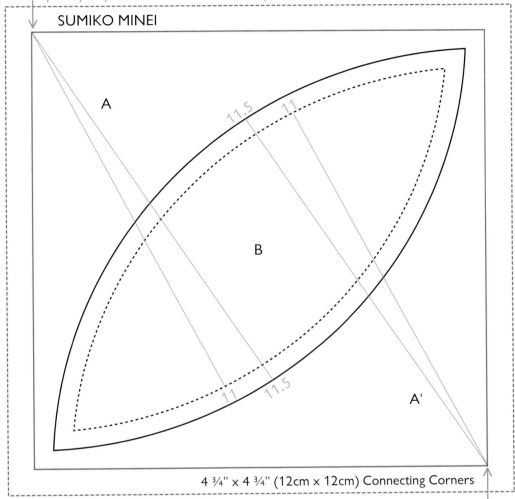

The place you put the circular attachment pin.

SUMIKO MINEI

A

11.5   11

B

11   11.5

A'

4 ¾" x 4 ¾" (12cm x 12cm) Connecting Corners

The place you put the circular attachment pin.

◆ When you use different colors for each piece:

A ...... $\dfrac{5¾" \times 5¾"}{2}$ ($\dfrac{14.5cm \times 14.5cm}{2}$) 1 piece

A' ..... $\dfrac{5¾" \times 5¾"}{2}$ ($\dfrac{14.5cm \times 14.5cm}{2}$) 1 piece

B ...... 3" x 6¾" (7.5cm x 17cm) 1 piece

Place fabrics A and A' right-sides together; sew both sides as shown in the figure and open the seam allowances. The center opening is for you to insert scissors when you trim away excess fabrics A and A'.

◆ When you use the same colors for some parts:

When you use the same color for A and A':

.............5¾" sq (14.5cm x 14.5cm) 1 piece

Fabric B is the same.

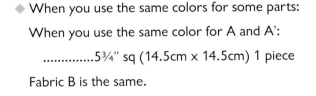

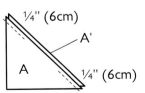

¼" (6cm)

A'

A

¼" (6cm)

DOUBLE WEDDING RING WITH TRADITIONAL CORNERS

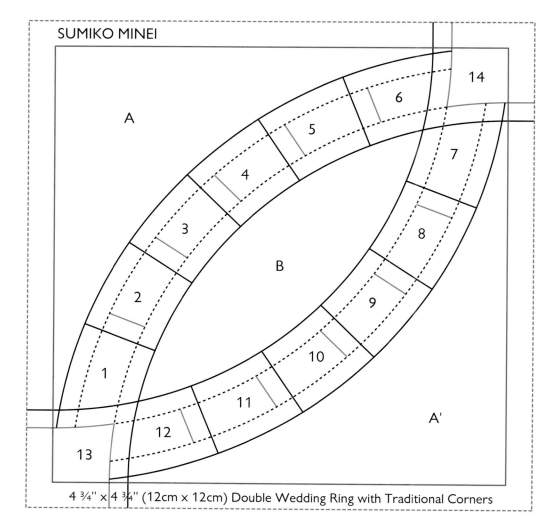

SUMIKO MINEI

A

14

6

5

4

7

3

8

B

2

9

1

10

11

13

12

A'

4 ¾" x 4 ¾" (12cm x 12cm) Double Wedding Ring with Traditional Corners

◆ When you use different colors for each piece:

A ...... $\dfrac{5¾" \times 5¾"}{2}$ $\left(\dfrac{14.5\text{cm} \times 14.5\text{cm}}{2}\right)$ 1 piece

A' ..... $\dfrac{5¾" \times 5¾"}{2}$ $\left(\dfrac{14.5\text{cm} \times 14.5\text{cm}}{2}\right)$ 1 piece

B ...... 2" x 5⅛" (5cm x 13cm) 1 piece

Pieces 1–12

...... 1⅝" x 1½" (4cm x 3.5cm) 1 piece each

Pieces 13–14

...... 1⅝" sq (4cm x 4cm) 1 piece each

* Be careful to position fabrics 1–12
  correctly (width and length).

◆ When you use the same colors for some parts:

When you use the same color for A, A' and B:

................5¾" sq (14.5cm x 14.5cm) 1 piece

Fabrics 1–14 are the same.

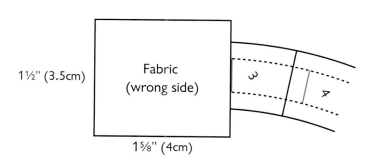

1½" (3.5cm)

Fabric
(wrong side)

3

4

1⅝" (4cm)

DOUBLE WEDDING RING WITH SQUARE CORNERS

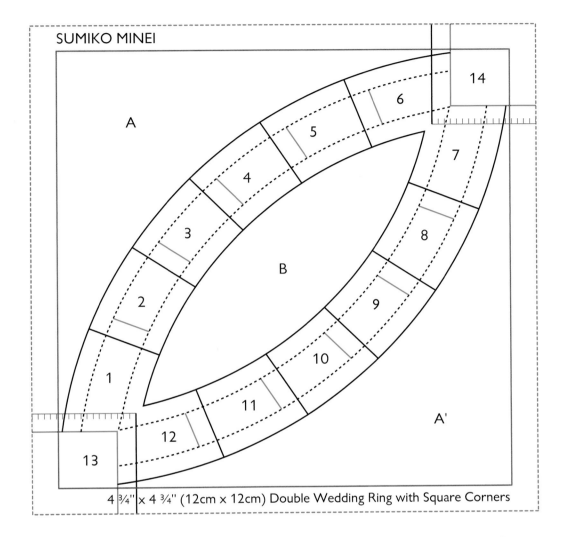

SUMIKO MINEI

A

14

6

5

4

7

3

B

8

2

9

1

10

11

A'

12

13

4 ¾" x 4 ¾" (12cm x 12cm) Double Wedding Ring with Square Corners

◆ When you use different colors for each piece:

A ...... $\frac{5¾" \times 5¾"}{2}$ ($\frac{14.5cm \times 14.5cm}{2}$) 1 piece

A' ..... $\frac{5¾" \times 5¾"}{2}$ ($\frac{14.5cm \times 14.5cm}{2}$) 1 piece

B ...... 2" x 5⅛" (5cm x 13cm) 1 piece

Pieces 1–12

...... 1⅝" x 1½" (4cm x 3.5cm) 1 piece each

Pieces 13–14

.... 1⅝" sq (4cm x 4cm) 1 piece each

◆ When you use the same colors for some parts:

When you use the same color for A, A' and B:

.................5¾" sq (14.5cm x 14.5cm) 1 piece

Fabrics 1–14 are the same.

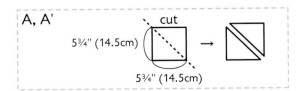

A, A'
cut
5¾" (14.5cm)
5¾" (14.5cm)

INDIAN WEDDING RING WITH TRADITIONAL CORNERS

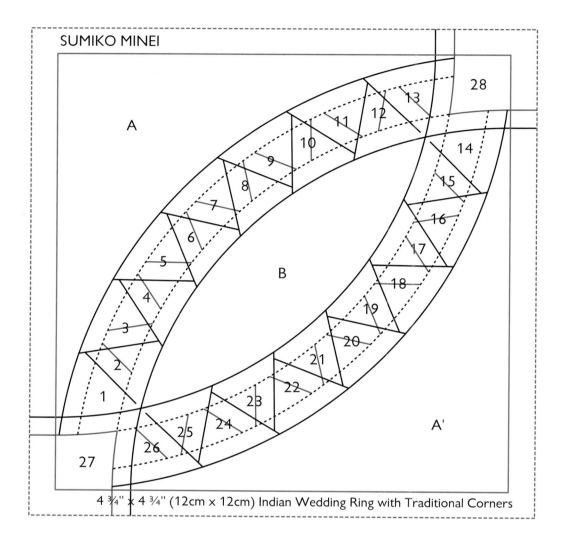

SUMIKO MINEI

A

28

13

12

11

10

9

14

8

15

7

16

6

17

5

B

18

4

19

3

20

2

21

1

22

A'

23

24

25

26

27

4 ¾" x 4 ¾" (12cm x 12cm) Indian Wedding Ring with Traditional Corners

◆ When you use different colors for each piece:

A ...... $\frac{5\frac{3}{4}" \times 5\frac{3}{4}"}{2}$ $\left(\frac{14.5cm \times 14.5cm}{2}\right)$ 1 piece

A' ..... $\frac{5\frac{3}{4}" \times 5\frac{3}{4}"}{2}$ $\left(\frac{14.5cm \times 14.5cm}{2}\right)$ 1 piece

B ...... 2" x 5⅛" (5cm x 13cm) 1 piece

Pieces 1–26

...... 1½" sq (3.5cm x 3.5cm) 1 piece each

Pieces 27–28

...... 1⅝" sq (4cm x 4cm) 1 piece each

◆ When you use the same colors for some parts:

When you use the same color for A, A' and B:

................5¾" sq (14.5cm x 14.5cm) 1 piece

Fabrics 1–28 are the same.

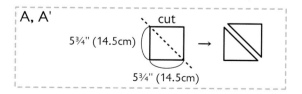

A, A'

cut

5¾" (14.5cm)

5¾" (14.5cm)

INDIAN WEDDING RING WITH SQUARE CORNERS

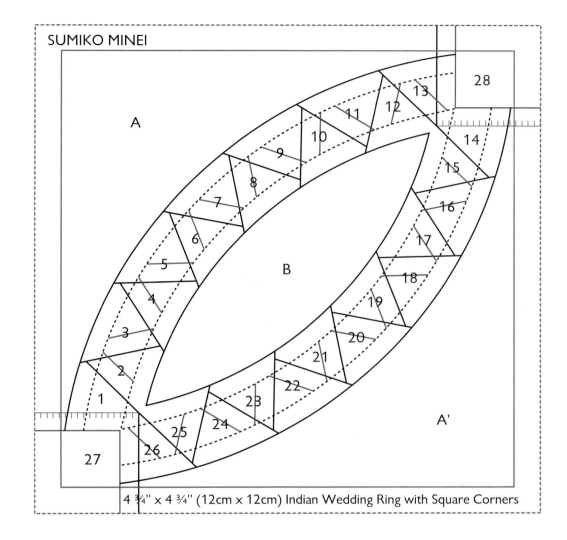

SUMIKO MINEI

4 ¾" x 4 ¾" (12cm x 12cm) Indian Wedding Ring with Square Corners

◆ When you use different colors for each piece:

A ...... $\frac{5¾" \times 5¾"}{2}$ ($\frac{14.5cm \times 14.5cm}{2}$) 1 piece

A' ..... $\frac{5¾" \times 5¾"}{2}$ ($\frac{14.5cm \times 14.5cm}{2}$) 1 piece

B ...... 2" x 5⅛" (5cm x 13cm) 1 piece

Pieces 1–26

...... 1½" sq (3.5cm x 3.5cm) 1 piece each

Pieces 27–28

...... 1⅝" sq (4cm x 4cm) 1 piece each

◆ When you use the same colors for some parts:

When you use the same color for A, A' and B:

.................5¾" sq (14.5cm x 14.5cm) 1 piece

Fabrics 1–28 are the same.

Quilting Patterns 1–3

You may use and adapt these three quilting designs in many ways:

◆ Use just part of any one design

◆ Mix and match parts of two or more of the designs

◆ Change the design size larger or smaller to fit your quilting area

THIS PAGE: SPRING APRIL, detail. Full quilt on page 31.

QUILTING PATTERN 1

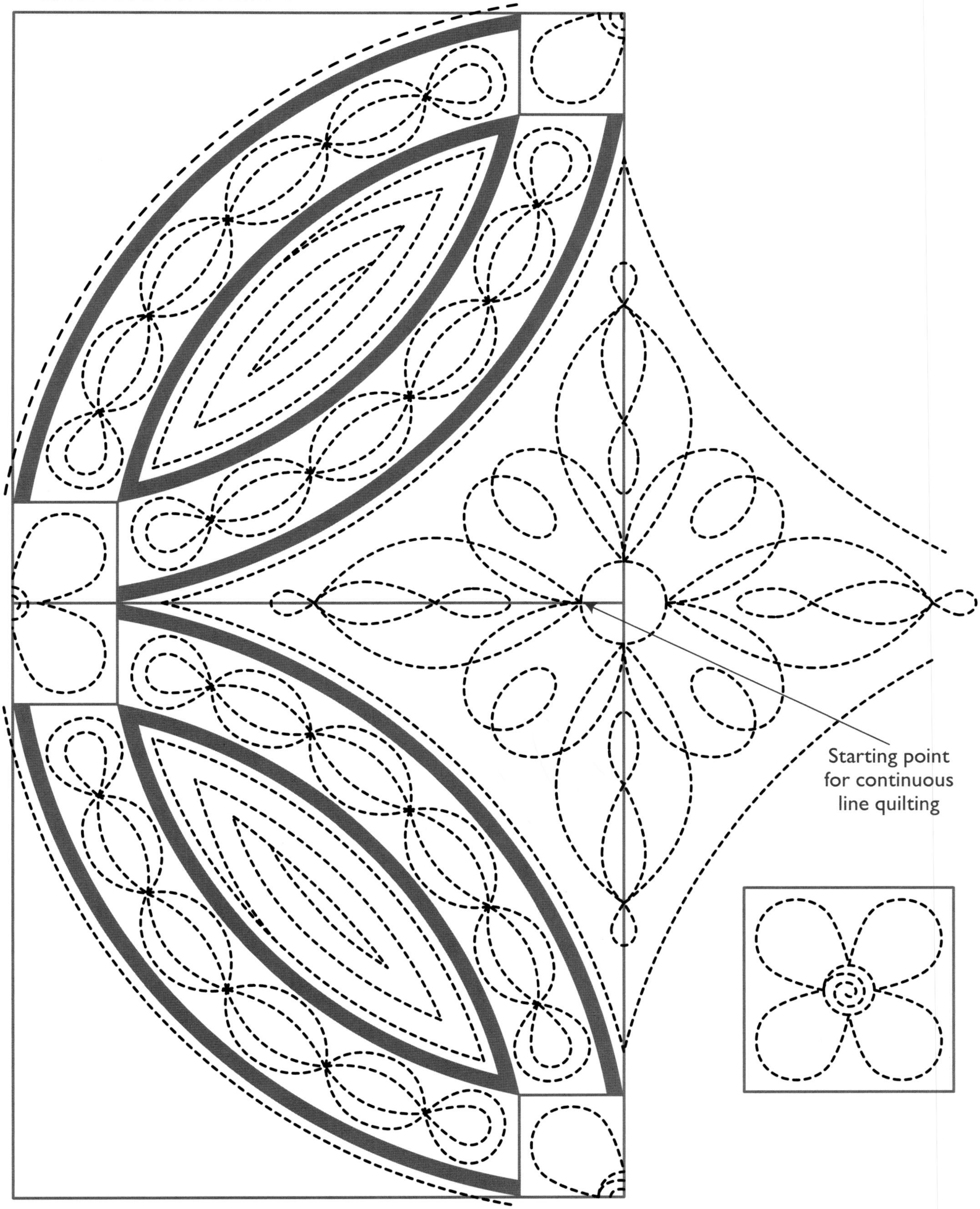

Starting point
for continuous
line quilting

QUILTING PATTERN 2

Starting point
for continuous
line quilting

QUILTING PATTERN 3

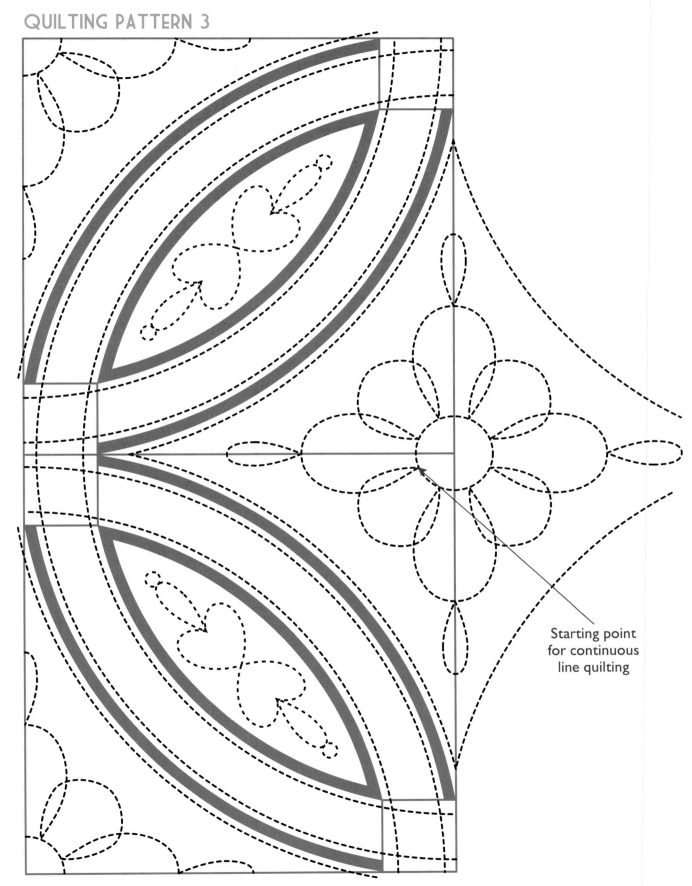

Starting point
for continuous
line quilting

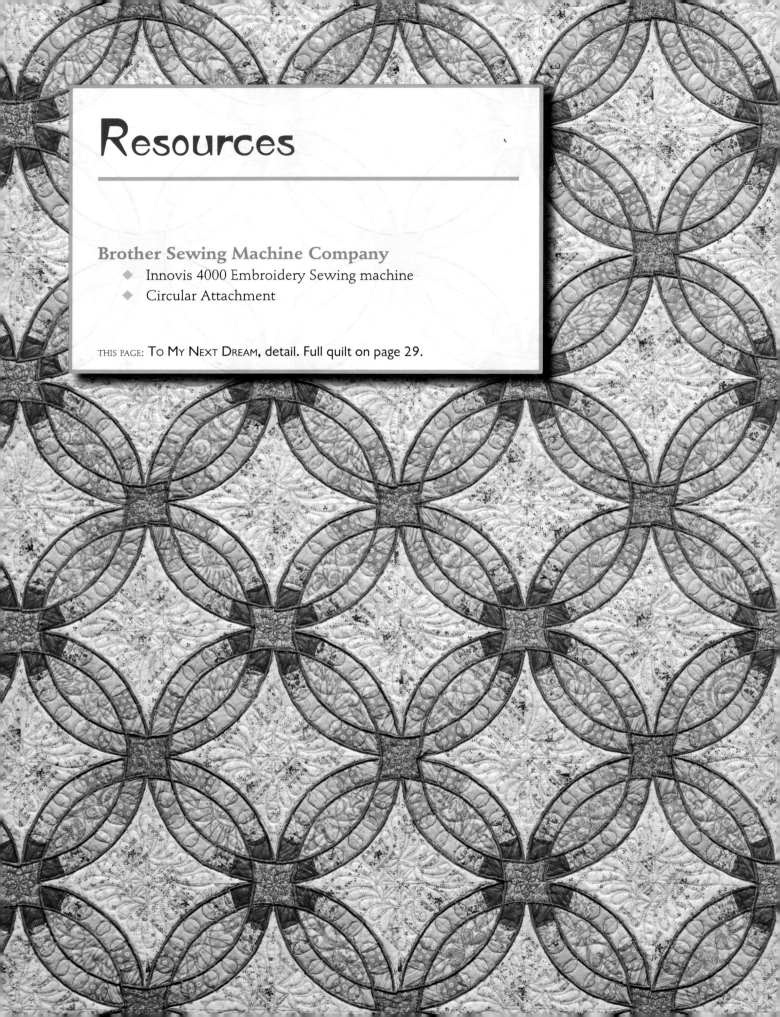

Resources

Brother Sewing Machine Company
- ◆ Innovis 4000 Embroidery Sewing machine
- ◆ Circular Attachment

THIS PAGE: TO MY NEXT DREAM, detail. Full quilt on page 29.

About the Author & Translator

ABOUT THE AUTHOR

Sumiko Minei was born in Toyama Prefecture located in the Hokuriku region on Honshù island, Japan. After working as a dietitian in hospitals, she quit her job upon marriage in 1971 and began making and teaching patchwork quilts, which she'd been interested in for a long time. In 1988 she took a workshop on machine quilting from Danita Rafalovich. Since then Sumiko has pursued the unlimited possibilities of making quilts by machine.

Many of her quilts have appeared in magazines and books and been accepted in many shows in Japan, the U.S., and Australia. She has taught quilting around Japan as well as in Korea, Hungary, and the U.S., including the Pacific International Quilt Festival.

Books by Sumiko include *Paper Foundation Piecing* (Patchwork Tsushin Co., Ltd, 1999); *Embroidery Machine Piecing & Appliqué, Vols. 1 & 2* (Brother, Ltd., 2008 & 2009); and *Foundation Piecing Patterns Vols. 1 & 2* (Tong Tong Quilts, 2009 & 2010).

She lives in Tokyo with her daughter, Megumi. Please visit
http://www.tongtongquilt.com/
(website is in Japanese).

AUTHOR: Sumiko Minei

ABOUT THE TRANSLATOR

Ayu Ohta was born in Tokyo and still lives there. She has loved needlework since her childhood; she began making quilts in 1982. Her quilts have been displayed in Japan, the U.S, Australia, England, France, Hungary, and Korea.

She has worked as a translator for *Patchwork Quilt Tsushin* magazine (Patchwork Tsushin Co., Ltd.), *Patchwork* magazine (Deagostini Japan) and the International Quilt Week Yokohama festival. In addition, Ayu has translated novels by Ruth Rendell and Ken Weber.

Learn more about Ayu at
http://www.h4.dion.ne.jp/~quilt/
(website is in Japanese).

TRANSLATOR: Ayu Ohta

more AQS Books

This is only a small selection of the books available from the American Quilter's Society. AQS books are known worldwide for timely topics, clear writing, beautiful color photos, and accurate illustrations and patterns. The following books are available from your local bookseller, quilt shop, or public library.

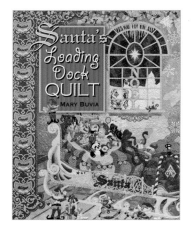

#8768

#8761

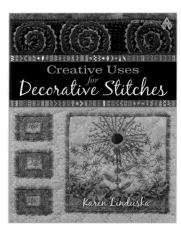

#8762

#8532

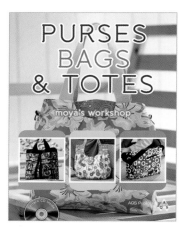

#8764

#8763

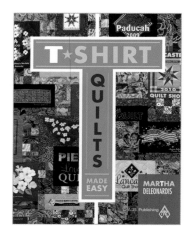

#8664

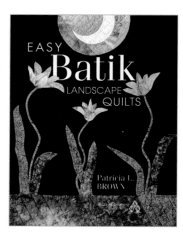

#8527

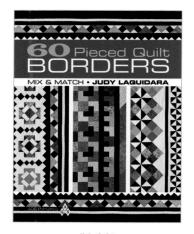

#8662